Date: 4/29/22

J BIO YOUSAFZAI
Schwartz, Heather E.,
Malala Yousafzai : heroic
education activist /

ALTERNATOR
BOOKS™

MALALA YOUSAFZAI

HEROIC EDUCATION ACTIVIST

HEATHER E. SCHWARTZ

Lerner Publications ◆ Minneapolis

Lerner Publications Company
An imprint of Lerner Publishing Group, Inc.
241 First Avenue North
Minneapolis, MN 55401 USA

For reading levels and more information, look up this title at www.lernerbooks.com.

Main body text set in Aptifer Sans LT Pro.
Typeface provided by Linotype AG.

Editor: Andrea Nelson **Designer:** Lindsey Owens

Library of Congress Cataloging-in-Publication Data

Names: Schwartz, Heather E., author.
Title: Malala Yousafzai : heroic education activist / Heather E. Schwartz.
Description: Minneapolis : Lerner Publications, 2021. | Series: Boss Lady Bios
    (Alternator Books) | Includes bibliographical references and index. | Audience:
    Ages 8–12 | Audience: Grades 4–6 | Summary: "Malala Yousafzai's activism has
    placed her in grave danger from the Taliban, but she remains determined to
    defend girls' right to an education. Follow Yousafzai from young blogger to
    Nobel Peace Prize recipient."—Provided by publisher.
Identifiers: LCCN 2019035039 (print) | LCCN 2019035040 (ebook) |
    ISBN 9781541597112 (library binding) | ISBN 9781541599697 (ebook)
Subjects: LCSH: Yousafzai, Malala, 1997– —Juvenile literature. | Girls—Education—
    Pakistan—Juvenile literature. | Girls—Violence against—Pakistan—Juvenile
    literature. | Women social reformers—Pakistan—Biography—Juvenile
    literature. | Taliban—Juvenile literature. | Pakistan—Social conditions—Juvenile
    literature.
Classification: LCC LC2330 .S39 2020 (print) | LCC LC2330 (ebook) |
    DDC 371.822095491—dc23

LC record available at https://lccn.loc.gov/2019035039
LC ebook record available at https://lccn.loc.gov/2019035040

Manufactured in the United States of America
1-47815-48255-11/18/2019

TABLE OF CONTENTS

Malala Yousafzai displays her medal and diploma during the 2014 Nobel Peace Prize award ceremony.

Den Norske Nobelkomite har overensstemmende med reglene i det av ALFRED NOBEL den 27. november 1895 opprettede testamente tildelt Malala Yousafzai Nobels Fredspris for 2014

Oslo 10. desember 2014

TAKING THE STAGE

MALALA YOUSAFZAI STEPPED ONSTAGE TO THUNDEROUS APPLAUSE. She smiled as the audience applause continued for her and fellow prizewinner Kailash Satyarthi during the Nobel Prize ceremony in the Oslo City Hall in Norway on December 10, 2014. The pair raised their medals in the air, and the crowd broke into cheers.

Seventeen-year-old Malala knew Satyarthi had been working for children's rights much longer than she'd been alive. His work was important and deserved recognition. It said a lot that the Nobel Committee wanted to recognize her own work as well.

Malala Yousafzai and Kailash Satyarthi accept the 2014 Nobel Peace Prize.

Malala Yousafzai delivers her acceptance speech during the Nobel Prize award ceremony.

But Malala's work wasn't about winning prizes. It was about making a difference. And her fight was far from over.

"This award is not just for me. It is for those forgotten children who want education," she said in her acceptance speech. "I am here to stand up for their rights, to raise their voice. . . . It is not time to pity them. It is time to take action."

GETTING IT DONE!

At seventeen years old, Malala became the youngest recipient of a Nobel Peace Prize.

YOU'RE THE BOSS

Giving speeches is a great way to influence others and gain support for your ideas. But speaking in front of a group can be hard or even scary. If you practice, you'll be more confident and comfortable when speaking in front of an audience.

Start by practicing speeches in private. Long before her Nobel Prize speech, Malala practiced her speeches in front of her bathroom mirror. Once you feel more comfortable, you can ask family members to be your audience. After that, you may be ready to speak to your class, grade, or entire school.

CHAPTER 1
GROWING UP

MALALA YOUSAFZAI WAS BORN ON JULY 12, 1997, IN THE SWAT VALLEY OF PAKISTAN. Growing up, she worried that her future was limited. Women in Pakistan weren't allowed to pursue certain types of careers, such as engineering or art. Most, including her own mother, Toor Pekai Yousafzai, were illiterate. Malala longed to be like her younger brothers, Khushal and Atal, who could reach for any career they dreamed of as adults.

But Malala's father, Ziauddin Yousafzai, ran several private schools and believed strongly in educating girls. Malala attended one of his schools, Khushal School, and every subject she studied excited her. With his support, Malala began to see that her world could be bigger than she'd imagined.

"WE GIRLS TRAVELED FAR AND WIDE INSIDE THE PAGES OF OUR BOOKS. IN A LAND WHERE MANY WOMEN CAN'T READ THE PRICES IN THE MARKETS, WE DID MULTIPLICATION," MALALA WROTE LATER. "WE DIDN'T KNOW WHERE OUR EDUCATION WOULD TAKE US. ALL WE WANTED WAS A CHANCE TO LEARN IN PEACE."

Malala and her friends enjoyed their time at school. But the world around them was beginning to change. Terrorist leader Mullah Fazlullah began to gain power in the Swat Valley. He joined with the Pakistan Taliban, a group that wanted to take away the rights of women and girls, among other things. In 2007, when Malala

Some Pakistani schools continued to teach girls despite threats from the Taliban.

Under the Talib
women were re
to cover their h
bodies when in
Eventually, they
allowed in publi

was ten, the Taliban declared that women were no longer allowed in public places and TVs were forbidden. This limited women's opportunities to get information about what was happening outside their homes. People who defied the Taliban were beaten and killed.

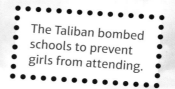
The Taliban bombed schools to prevent girls from attending.

CHAPTER 2
SPEAKING OUT

MALALA'S SCHOOL STAYED OPEN, BUT FEARFUL STUDENTS BEGAN TO DROP OUT. Teachers left too. The Taliban threatened her father for educating girls. But he didn't close the school, even when the Taliban began bombing other schools. Despite the ongoing violence, Malala was determined to continue her education.

"Every morning, before I rounded the corner on the way to the Khushal School, I closed my eyes and said a prayer—afraid to open them in case the school had been reduced to rubble overnight. This was what terrorism felt like," Malala wrote later.

In December 2008, the Taliban announced that starting on January 15, 2009, all girls were forbidden to attend school. Students, parents, and even school principals had no way to fight back. The Taliban was too powerful and dangerous to disobey.

Kushal School

Malala was upset. She couldn't imagine what her life would become without an education. The future she imagined for herself would be impossible.

But Malala discovered she could make a difference. She learned that her father was trying to help a friend at the BBC (British Broadcasting Corporation). The BBC wanted someone to blog about life under Taliban rule. Everyone the BBC had approached was scared. But Malala wasn't.

BBC headquarters in London, United Kingdom

Malala began writing for the BBC when she was just eleven years old.

Malala agreed to write about living under the Taliban and her efforts to receive an education. The BBC gave her a pseudonym—Gul Makai—to protect her identity. The BBC published Malala's first entry on January 3, 2009. She started by writing about how scary life was. She explained that she had trouble studying and sleeping because she could hear fighting outside. Then she wrote about how much she cherished getting

GETTING IT DONE

In 2011 Malala won Pakista first National Peace Prize f work on the BBC blog.

an education. Even though she was scared of being followed or attacked on her way to school, she proudly wore her school uniform. People all over the world read her words. Malala gave interviews locally, going on TV to speak up. The *New York Times* even made a documentary about her experience. She spoke on camera about her determination to get her education no matter what.

Malala was scared that the Taliban would try to silence her for speaking out, but that did not stop her from standing up to injustice.

YOU'RE THE BOSS

Malala used words to fight injustice. You can do the same. If you don't know what to do about a problem, write about it. Make it an essay or an article for your school or community newspaper. You could even start a blog. Tell readers what is happening and how you feel about it. If you have ideas about how to solve the problem, include those too.

Even if you don't have a solution, writing can help. Your words will call attention to the problem. They'll inspire others to get involved and figure out what to do.

CHAPTER 3
FIGHTING BACK

BY 2012 MALALA WAS FAMOUS FOR REFUSING TO KEEP QUIET AND GIVE IN TO THE TALIBAN. But early that year, the terrorists decided to silence her. Malala was influencing people, and she was a threat to their power in the Swat Valley.

One day her father showed her a death threat from the Taliban. Malala was calm. "The worst had happened. I had been targeted by the Taliban," she wrote later. "Now I would get back to doing what I was meant to do."

But in October, the Taliban moved beyond threatening words. Malala was riding the bus home from school with her friends when the vehicle suddenly stopped on a quiet street. Armed men boarded the bus, and one asked if it was coming from Khushal School. He asked which girl was Malala. Then he shot her in the head.

The bus driver sped to the hospital. The next thing Malala knew, she was waking up in a foreign hospital. She didn't know it yet, but she'd had surgery and had

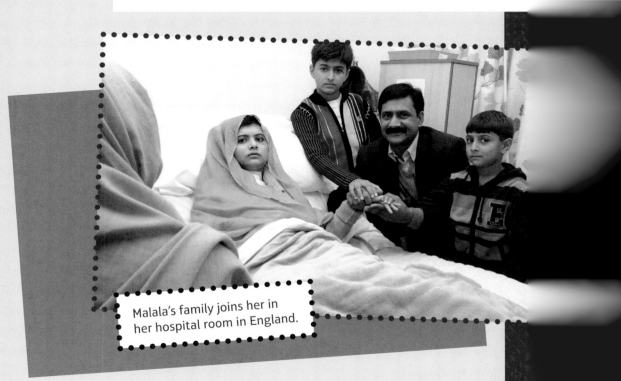

Malala's family joins her in her hospital room in England.

Pakistani students carry posters with Malala's face on them during a protest against the Taliban on October 16, 2012.

almost died before her transfer to England for more care. She spent the next several days confused and in pain as doctors worked to help her.

As Malala recovered, she learned that support for her cause had grown greatly. Her family had always stood by her. And politicians and journalists were asking to meet with her. The president of Pakistan visited. Celebrities like Selena Gomez, Beyoncé, and Angelina Jolie reached out with messages.

"The Taliban shot me to try to silence me," she wrote later. "Instead, the whole world was listening to my message now."

She had faced death and survived. The Taliban warned they would try to kill Malala again. But her story had spread across the globe. Nothing could stop her.

Pakistani girls show their support for Malala after the attempt on her life.

CHAPTER 4
MOVING FORWARD

Malala Yousafzai leaves Queen Elizabeth Hospital in Birmingham, England.

WHEN MALALA WAS WELL ENOUGH TO LEAVE THE HOSPITAL, IT WAS TOO DANGEROUS FOR HER FAMILY TO RETURN HOME. She had to start a new life in Birmingham, England. Malala's new school had computers and special classes that she'd always longed for in Pakistan. But she was lonely for her friends in Pakistan and still wished for better educational opportunities for them. So Malala kept up her activism, working through the loneliness that sometimes set in. She knew her work was too important to quit.

"SOME DAYS I WISH I COULD JUST SIT ON THE COUCH . . . OR SKYPE WITH FRIENDS. BUT I TAKE THE WORK I'M DOING VERY SERIOUSLY, ALWAYS," SHE SAID. "MY LIFE HAS BECOME EXTREMELY BUSY. I AM MAKING BOOKS, DOCUMENTARIES, AND SPEECHES, AND I AM MEETING INTERESTING PEOPLE, DOING SOCIAL MEDIA CAMPAIGNS, AND ENGAGING IN HUMANITARIAN WORK."

I Am Malala became a worldwide best seller.

Malala's work gained momentum when she released her book *I Am Malala* in 2013 and won the Nobel Peace Prize in 2014. In 2017 she became a United Nations Messenger of Peace. She also received honorary Canadian citizenship. And in 2018 she finally returned to Pakistan to meet with the prime minister.

GETTING IT DONE!

Malala and her father founded the Malala Fund in 2013. The focus is support for every girl's right to twelve years of free, safe, quality education.

Malala has won fame and many awards for her work, but her activism was never about her own personal gain. She continues to focus on others and the world. In 2019 she released *We Are Displaced*, a book of true stories of refugee girls.

"People have heard my story already," she said. "I thought it was time for people to listen to other girls' stories as well."

The Malala Fund has helped to support schools in Syrian refugee camps so that girls can continue their education.

Even with her life in danger, Malala has never been afraid to speak up for her own rights and the rights of others. She felt too strongly about her message to remain silent.

Malala gives the keynote speech during the World Assembly for Women conference on March 23, 2019, in Tokyo, Japan.

Malala continues to travel around the world in support of education rights for girls.

She is sure to continue making change happen in the world.

TIMELINE

- July 12, 1997   Malala is born in the Swat Valley of Pakistan.

- Late 2007   The Taliban takes control of the Swat Valley.

- January 3, 2009   Malala's first blog entry appears on the BBC.

- January 15, 2009   The Taliban bans girls from attending school.

- October 2012   Malala is shot by the Taliban.

- October 8, 2013   She releases her book *I Am Malala*.

- December 10, 2014   She becomes the youngest person to win the Nobel Peace Prize.

- 2019   Her book *We Are Displaced* is released.

GLOSSARY

activism: taking strong action or supporting strong actions to help make changes in politics or society

citizenship: the fact or status of being a citizen of a particular place

documentary: a movie or television program that tells the facts about actual people and events

honorary: regarded as one of a group although not officially included

illiterate: not knowing how to read or write

pseudonym: a name used to hide a person's identity

refugee: someone who has been forced to leave a country because of war or for religious or political reasons

terrorist: a person who uses or supports the use of terrorism, such as bombing or threats

SOURCE NOTES

6   Malala Yousafzai, "Malala Yousafzai: Nobel Peace Prize Acceptance Speech," Malala Fund, December 10, 2014, https://www.malala.org/newsroom /malala-nobel-speech?gclid=Cj0KCQjwyLDpBRCxAR IsAEENsrKsEJzvAcnlb-c8YMDPNqRcXHEluIPRGCcmp YxNXgvE6r5ki6GTBZgaAtF2EALw_wcB.

9   Malala Yousafzai and Patricia McCormick, *I Am Malala* (New York: Little, Brown, 2014), 34–35.

13   Yousafzai and McCormick, 65.

19   Yousafzai and McCormick, 118.

21   Yousafzai and McCormick, 164.

23   Yousafzai and McCormick, 180.

25   Lisa Allerdice, "Malala Yousafzai on Student Life, Facing Critics—and her Political Ambitions," *Guardian* (US edition), January 19, 2019, https://www.theguardian.com/books/2019/jan/19/malala -yousafzai-voice-generation-we-are-displaced.

LEARN MORE

Doeden, Matt. *Malala Yousafzai: Shot by the Taliban, Still Fighting for Equal Education*. Minneapolis: Lerner Publications, 2015.

Jeffries, Joyce. *Who Are Refugees?* New York: KidHaven, 2018.

Malala Fund
https://www.malala.org

The Nobel Prize
https://www.nobelprize.org/

Plan International: Youth Activism
https://plan-international.org/youth-activism

Schatz, Kate. *Rad Girls Can: Stories of Bold, Brave, and Brilliant Young Women*. Berkeley, CA: Ten Speed, 2018.

The United Nations: Students
https://www.un.org/en/sections/resources-different
-audiences/students/index.html

Yousafzai, Malala. *Malala: My Story of Standing Up for Girls' Rights*. New York: Little, Brown, 2018.

INDEX

PHOTO ACKNOWLEDGMENTS

Image credits: ODD ANDERSEN/AFP/Getty Images, p. 4; Nigel Waldron/Stringer/Getty Images, pp. 5, 6; Amir Mukhtar/Getty Images, p. 8; Vivien Killilea/Getty Images, p. 9; Veronique de Viguerie/Getty Images, pp. 10, 11, 23, 16; RASHID MAHMOOD/AFP/Getty Images, p. 13; WILL OLIVER/AFP/Getty Images, pp. 14, 15; Saeed Shah/MCT/Tribune News Service/Getty Images, p. 18; Queen Elizabeth Hospital/Getty Images, pp. 19, 22; ARIF ALI/Getty Images, p. 20; RIZWAN TABASSUM/Getty Images, p. 21; Sean Drakes/Getty Images, p. 24; picture alliance/Getty Images, p. 25; The Asahi Shimbun/Getty Images, p. 26; FRANCK ROBICHON/Getty Images, p. 27.

Cover images: Louise Kennerley/Fairfax Media/Getty Images.